Affiliate Marketing Guide

David Steele

Published by RWG Publishing, 2021.

While every precaution has been taken in the preparation of this book, the publisher assumes no responsibility for errors or omissions, or for damages resulting from the use of the information contained herein.

AFFILIATE MARKETING GUIDE

First edition. July 14, 2021.

Copyright © 2021 David Steele.

Written by David Steele.

Table of Contents

Utilizing Clickbank as an Affiliate Marketing Career Launch Pad .. 1

Investigating Why There Is Ease in Starting Affiliate Marketing Ventures 3

Article Directories Really Help In Affiliate Marketing 5

Rules for Creating a Superior Affiliate Marketing Website 7

The most effective method to Choose the Best Affiliate Program 9

Pay Increase Tips For Affiliate Marketers 11

Is It Possible To Pocket A Six Figure Income Through Affiliate Marketing? 13

Finding Top Affiliate Marketing Programs 15

Spam Complaints and How to Avoid Them in Affiliate Marketing 17

The Definition of Affiliate Marketing and What It Entails 19

The Effect That Blogging Has On Affiliate Marketing 21

The Importance of Mailing Lists in Affiliate Marketing 23

The Sure Way to Boost Your Niche Affiliate Marketing Business .. 25

Composing Quality Keyword Rich Articles for Affiliate Marketing 27

Utilizing Link Building to Market Your Affiliate Website 29

Utilizing Social Networking to Market Your Affiliate Site 31

Week after week, Bi-Weekly, Or Monthly: Which Affiliate Pay Structure Is Best 33

Utilizing Clickbank as an Affiliate Marketing Career Launch Pad

Subsidiary advertising is a feasible method to make great pay from commissions acquired in the wake of selling items and administrations for a business. Numerous individuals have proceeded to make great salaries from this movement having begun from pretty humble beginnings. For the fledgling who wishes to get into member advertising realizing where to begin can be exceptionally difficult. Clickbank may simply be your platform into this vocation in the event that you are keen on managing data items.

As one of the greatest data item commercial centers online Clickbank has end up being an incredible member promoting stage in any event, for the amateurs in the exchange. Clickbank bargains in the buy and offer of in excess of 30,000 data items. You can chip away at Clickbank as either a merchant or a partner. As a member you will be needed to sell the instructive items that the merchants have made.

For the subject of conversation close by we will consider the stuff to be a partner advertiser on Clickbank. To get going you should enroll or join. Similar as what occurs in different sites you will be needed to pick an ID that you will utilize each time you sign in. with this ID set up you would now be able to get to the Clickbank commercial center and test the items which you can sell. Clickbank have masterminded the commercial center in classifications of items which makes it simple for you to choose what you feel well on the way to sell. You can pick a solitary thing or a few.

Having chosen the product(s) the subsequent stage will be to procure a 'Hoplink' that will be utilized to guide imminent clients to the important seller deals page. The 'Hoplink' appears as a HTML code which is just created after your client ID is gone into an essential structure. Since every item that you need to sell has its own 'Hoplink' you may wind up with a lot. Clickbank members ordinarily record these hoplinks, deals page connections, and item data for simple reference. To sell the Clickbank items that you have chosen you simply need to have the hoplinks contribution to the business material.

Being a seller isn't troublesome all things considered. You simply need to have an item and pay a sum to have it recorded on the commercial center. Before the item is sold it must be Clickbank endorsed.

Investigating Why There Is Ease in Starting Affiliate Marketing Ventures

Dissimilar to numerous different organizations where getting going is truly hard member promoting enjoys some unmistakable benefits that have made it extremely famous with many yearning on the web business people. This is one of only a handful few organizations where you can begin procuring a good pay even for the time being.

Maybe the best benefit there is to member promoting has to do with the way that there are prepared items which you can begin selling right away. We as a whole like that it is so hard to concoct another item and have it become fruitful with the end goal that you make a nice pay from your creation. In partner showcasing you decide to sell items that you make certain of being effective with and the scope of these is huge and fluctuated.

Many new companies struggle with regards to issues of gathering installments after deals are made. Offshoot advertisers are not influenced by this as their subsidiary shippers do all the assortment from the clients.

In partner showcasing every advertiser is given an offshoot site by the vendor for whose sake the promoting is being finished. These sites are exclusively signed into with the end goal that all exchanges which are made there are credited to the subsidiary advertiser. It is basically impossible that that you can be denied of your duty.

Member promoting is tied in with showcasing - period. As an advertiser you are not worried about inventories and stock taking and different complexities of traditional organizations like conveyance and delivery. Your assignment is simply to sell the item and the trader then, at that point accepts accountability for getting the bought thing to the client.

The scope of associate promoting is generally amazing. You can essentially offer items to any area on earth gave there is a web association. Dissimilar to regular organizations where the customer base is confined to a city or a nation offshoot showcasing implies that the business exertion is worldwide. With member showcasing you don't have to stress over exchange limitations that administer various nations. A few items particularly the educational kind just necessitate that the client has a web association and a PC for downloading purposes.

One benefit that additionally stands apart unmistakably has to do with the actual Internet. The web is open day in and day out 365 and likewise your associate showcasing site additionally is. Regardless of where you are and paying little heed to the time you can generally expect that somebody some place can give you business.

Article Directories Really Help In Affiliate Marketing

Member advertisers must know about every one of the assets available to them that they can use for their organizations potential benefit. Business advantage in this setting alludes to the capacity of the dare to charm itself to both existent and forthcoming customer base.

Partner advertising starts from the decision of item that you need to sell. In the wake of choosing an item and a client specialty the time has come to consider what strategies will be utilized to produce deals page traffic. There several strategies that can be utilized for this reason including SEO and email showcasing. The adaptable subsidiary advertiser will anyway try to utilize a free strategy known as article showcasing. Through article showcasing many partner advertisers have had the option to acquire huge traffic and lovely remunerating awards for sure.

Many offshoot advertisers are taking up article composing and accommodation in perception of the advantages that can be gathered from doing as such. Prepared articles are submitted to article registries where they are distributed upon their wonderful of expressed essentials. It is pleasing that few out of every odd advertiser can be a capable essayist particularly when the article requires the inclusion of specific catchphrases. Regardless the member advertiser has a showcasing position to deal with. The person is in an ideal situation recruiting an article essayist to do the work and afterward appreciate the expanded volume of traffic for seemingly forever.

With accommodation registries one should comprehend that they are as of now all around put in web crawlers. This is a gigantic aid for partner advertisers and in light of current circumstances. An article that has been solid and steady as far as watchword inclusion and thickness will without a doubt be positioned exceptionally which converts into more viewership. With expanded viewership it is additionally truly likely that this will be converted into deals.

One thing that should be exceptionally clear about the composition of these articles is with respect to the substance. The ideal article offers the peruser much looked for data about the item specialty region and not simply the item essentially. This is the data that the peruser will go through and ideally settle on a choice with respect to whether the item merits purchasing. Articles that have been put in catalogs have asset boxes where data about the offshoot advertiser and the associate item deal site connect is embedded. Make the article subtleties as intriguing as conceivable to guarantee that the peruser goes right to the base where the asset box is.

Rules for Creating a Superior Affiliate Marketing Website

Your endeavors as a member advertiser ought to be guided towards drawing in online rush hour gridlock to your site and not the other way around. This is the reason the site you plan for this exertion ought to cling to fundamental rules that are known to be traffic-accommodating.

Clearness, cognizance and consistence are the fundamental things that you might want your site to be known for. The guest should have the option to quickly have an idea with regards to what you have on proposal as this will convince that person to peruse on.

The site you have as a top priority ought to be intended to be interesting to the objective imminent customers. The term 'engaging' can be misinterpreted to imply that the site ought to be loaded with enhanced visualizations and other like augmentations. In business, a site that is lumbering to those attempting to get to it doesn't gain the ideal ground. Best to have a site will establish a decent connection from the beginning. Pick your tones and text styles carefully just as the tone of language utilized. Guarantee that you speak with guests in way that will persuade them to work with you.

Close by the issues of importance as have been referenced over the site ought to be not difficult to utilize. While some level of intricacy is fine contingent upon the items and administrations that are being offered being additional complex isn't prudent. What guests like most in a site is the nature of content. This is normal for a portion of the more effective sites we have around.

While planning a site you ought to have the attitude of a client whether the person is a standard purchaser or a possibility. The site ought to however much as could be expected make the guest's experience wonderful for whatever that the person needs to do. Give specific consideration to issues of requesting and thing show. The site ought not contain what you believe is best for the traffic – the substance ought to be educated by genuine client slants.

An effective site consolidates great plan with amazing route. Route includes the utilization of connections that lead to a website page where wanted substance is to be found. Connections ought to in this way be very much meant so a guest can know where the snap will prompt. Close by route it is fundamental that a site is routinely refreshed. Access and download speeds are likewise basic to a site's prominence.

The most effective method to Choose the Best Affiliate Program

Prior to picking any subsidiary program you should explore and find the best and utilize something similar by advancing them before your rivals catch wind of them. Right now your rivals begin to understand the current member program, you ought to be as of now bringing in cash from the following executioner item. The general benefit of the best offshoot programs is that they assist a person with getting more cash on the web.

A few offshoots select some unacceptable projects to advance which as a rule restricts their capacity to make a decent pay. Essentially there is no particular best subsidiary promoting program except for what you do all relies upon the business sectors that you decide to engage with. It is very easy to pick the subsidiary program in that out of the web showcasing an individual will discover a chance to ride on the rear of the item dispatch and the promotion that it makes. While going through the destinations like Commission Junction among others, generally take a gander at the things that are selling the most and acquire the best.

Such items as of now have a demonstrated history and will empower you make some better memories spent in taking a gander at various points to draw in purchasing traffic other than investing your energy in testing the new member offers in order to see whether they will change over as you may anticipate. As a rule, the subsidiary items and administrations offers that are selling the most likewise have the best deals pages as the site proprietor has effectively done extensive testing to accomplish the best change rates the person requires.

It is in every case best to track down the right traffic and send it somewhere else where you as an individual know your shots at bringing in cash are higher by and large. An associate advantages in that the individual is paid for every single client or customer overcame their work. Any time a customer buys the assistance or item, bit of the benefit got from that specific exchange is credited to the subsidiaries account. This is saved as a commission. As a rule, the pay sum depends on fixed incentive for each visit or each enlistment. With regards to subsidiary advertising, the shipper's advantages on a more extensive spot to sell their administrations and products which draws in a lot of clients subsequently, expanded deals.

Pay Increase Tips For Affiliate Marketers

Partner advertising has for quite a while been viewed as a definitive large pay making vocation and it is this misperception that has truly startled numerous beginners. The truth is that there is no such vocation in presence and assuming there were, it would have effectively been outside the field of play for a lot.

Like any remaining vocations and occupations subsidiary showcasing is about difficult work and having the opportunity to get familiar with everything bit by bit. This is the mantra that partner advertiser learners should live by on the grounds that the underlying experience is a long way from the ruddy picture that has been made of the exchange. In fact numerous individuals have stopped their normal positions and set out on offshoot promoting. While some have fared on truly well some have been baffled by the top level salary illusion.

In offshoot showcasing there is no ensured approach to follow to make the major league salary that is wanted by many. The methodology that one member advertiser receives and gets fruitful with isn't really the very one that another advertiser will thrive with. Member showcasing is a greater amount of an individual methodology since it is you who understands what your clients like through the correspondence you share. The methodology that you use in the at first will require some tweaking of sorts with respect to the real factors on the ground. The business climate wherever is exceptionally unique and the best individuals are the ones who are prepared to adjust to these progressions by being inventive. It is tied in with understanding the requests and wishes of the traffic you experience and afterward offering precisely what suits them.

Associate advertisers can't bear to be uninformed about necessary subtleties like inert grammar and SEO. Master information on the utilization of catchphrases and the way in which they work is of substance. Every one of these are basic to guaranteeing that web search tools work for your potential benefit. Offshoot advertisers once in a while thrive without having their own sites and websites. Here the significance of watchword expresses in making content rich data again goes to the front. Such are the essential things one has to know whether great pay is to be made.

Seeing that singular exertion tallies nothing beats insight. You adapt a lot more by alluding from those who've been in the field longer. This is another method of saying that industry systems administration ought to likewise be viewed appropriately.

Is It Possible To Pocket A Six Figure Income Through Affiliate Marketing?

By and large the ones who own the sites and do not have the items or the administrations of their own to showcase, it's anything but a hard undertaking to bring in cash through the web. It is feasible to sell space for promoting however you need to draw in a few group to your site. You should draw in enormous rush hour gridlock to sell the promoting space. In the event that you don't do as such, you can't have the option to bring in any cash from anyone to allow you to publicize their destinations. On the off chance that you are sparsely ready to draw in enormous rush hour gridlock to your site and you don't have labor and products to sell, your answer is the six figure pay program.

In the six figure pay program, the creator instructs a person on the best way to procure at the very least 1,000 dollars each day yearly. The benefit of the six figure pay program is that the writer is prepared to help a person in each move he takes. As a rule, most advertisers like to begin bringing in cash from home as low maintenance premise. A large portion of the sites rely upon offshoot advertising to empower them acquire a great deal of deals since it's anything but a basic idea.

What offshoot showcasing for the most part involves is selling of others' labor and products for a commission which ranges between 5 to 25 percent of the item cost. The mystery is to change the traffic over to deals by ensuring that the labor and products you are advertising on your own site focus on your guests and target bunch. You ought to likewise guarantee that your adverts don't look like ordinary ads. This is so on the grounds that numerous individuals don't require some investment to focus on the flags that are dispersed all over however they do visit your site for data on what you give.

At the point when you are looking for an item as a member you need to take a gander at certain sites that sell the labor and products that are identified with your site's data. The greater part of these sites contain member programs and consistently have a connection that is put on their site remembering the data for how an individual can join to go along with them as a subsidiary. Fundamentally, subsidiary advertisers consistently appreciate the advantage of working for themselves and they work time permitting.

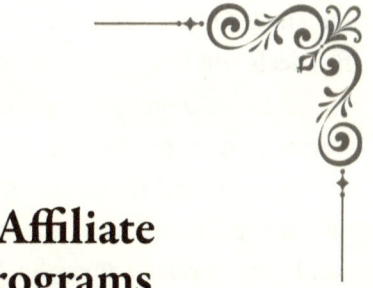

Finding Top Affiliate Marketing Programs

Offshoot advertising programs have large amounts of the web and in the event that you are in the hunt of a decent one, you will be spoilt for decision. This is anything but a simple insult; there are in a real sense a few large number of choices which you can investigate. Similarly as with everything accessible online there are acceptable and awful choices with regards to partner advertising programs. A portion of the projects will work to your advantage and others will not be so useful.

The fundamental thought that numerous potential offshoot advertisers are truly worried about is the measure of cash that they remain to acquire from their endeavors. The commissions that these partner promoting programs offer is very fluctuated. The most lucrative projects offer as much as 20 to 25 percent on every item that is sold through an advertiser's connections. For such projects business can be great since they typically sell items that are immensely famous across the globe.

The second most significant thought that is utilized as a determination model by associate advertisers has to do with the standing that the program appreciates. You will not turn out badly with a program that is perceived the world over just like a market chief. Clients then again likewise search for brand names that they perceive. Being an offshoot advertiser on a program like Western Union will undoubtedly be fruitful consistently simply as a result of the worldwide acknowledgment. Pick a program that appreciates numerous positive references on the grounds that the assignment of changing over these into deals will not be excessively troublesome.

Like the point just referenced about the altruism related with a specific partner promoting program is the thought about the items sold in that. A typical trademark that the greater part of the top subsidiary advertising sites share is the way that they offer items that bear truly well known brand names. Such brand names ingrain loads of certainty into forthcoming clients and surprisingly the all around existing ones. It is irrefutable that these items sell most and an associate advertiser who offers such is certainly going to acquire solid returns.

Partner showcasing programs have various methods of managing their offshoots. A member advertiser will improve working with a program that has lovely acquiring motivating forces like commissions for item advancement through promotions on the offshoot's site. Conceded that joining a large number of these subsidiary showcasing programs is free it will not do any harm on the off chance that you have a go at doing as such.

Spam Complaints and How to Avoid Them in Affiliate Marketing

The fruitful subsidiary advertiser has a considerable endorser list that the person in question can depend upon for supported business even in lean occasions. The principles of partner showcasing direct that to keep up with such a rundown there must be correspondence between the two gatherings. The endorsers expect that you will be in ordinary contact with them by circling back to their requests and remarks. This correspondence is ordinarily through email. Endorsers opposed spam mail and as a subsidiary advertiser you should ensure that you don't get spam grievances from any of your supporters. Spam is an issue that gives offshoot promoting a truly downright terrible and you essentially can't permit this to destroy a generally energetic endeavor.

There are basic things that you can do to guarantee your business is spam objection free. Regardless you should focus on the believability of the data that you furnish your clients with. Whatever the organization of data you offer them (this can be sound, video, or composed) you ought to guarantee that it is verifiable and dependable. For a business where you can't generally make facial contact your validity is estimated upon the substance you offer. For this matter you can't stand to have indiscriminately pre-arranged material on your site. All that the supporters read should tell them you are a dependable master in the assigned region.

Clients place their trust in the item or administration you are selling just in light of the fact that you said as much. This assertion may be substantial however it doesn't at all imply that the clients will simply buy anything. The truth is that the Internet is likewise host to a major number of
sham items and not all forthcoming clients are sufficiently artless to be influenced into buying such. As the subsidiary advertiser you are relied upon to have done your statistical surveying admirably ahead of time to try not to wind up with some major embarrassment. You should actually vet the items you are selling in order to make an educated proposal to the clients.

Keeping fixed at work is an issue that is basic to any business not to mention member promoting. With center you will be reliably persistent even in the smallest of subtleties. Organizations develop with time if the functioning norms are kept up with exceptionally. With this at the rear of your brain your subsidiary promoting adventure won't be a failure.

The Definition of Affiliate Marketing and What It Entails

Expanded business contest on a worldwide scale has taken off to remarkable rates especially over the most recent couple of years. Every single business has an aim of accomplishing economies of scale and this is principally done through a decrease of costs at every possible opportunity.

Promoting is the methods by which organizations get their items into the client domain. It is the methods through which imminent customers are sharpened about the accessibility of items that they need or which they may require. Promoting is anything but a modest exertion particularly when you consider the media through which it is finished. Of late numerous organizations have been utilizing the Internet as a promoting medium. Partner promoting is one of the structures through which this is done and it has end up being both modest and viable.

In offshoot promoting the concerned business has an affiliate(s) whose work it is to lead clients toward the said business. The business then, at that point compensates its offshoots for each customer that was landed on account of the endeavors of the members. A business may have offshoots as the executives organizations, associate administrators, and partner organizations. It is these members who direct web advertising in the interest of the business and in this manner advance the labor and products that they offer.

Subsidiary advertisers have some picked apparatuses of exchange that they use in the promoting exertion. A portion of the more normal procedures generally utilized in associate showcasing incorporate Search Engine Optimization (SEO), web crawler advertising, and email promoting.

In the developmental days of this advertising procedure labor and products were frequently advanced through spam. This has anyway changed to the making of pages. The site pages are enhanced for web search tool positioning using specialty watchwords. A streamlined website page will without a doubt prompt more webpage traffic and accordingly the help or item being elevated will be presented to a more prominent crowd. Getting sufficient traffic for a built site can be really difficult. It is the SEO methods that are generally utilized in guaranteeing that an ever increasing number of individuals are made mindful about the site.

Offshoot promoting is yet to accomplish its maximum capacity however its ubiquity is on the ascent particularly after the advertisers began shunning utilizing spam. The upsides of associate advertising are anyway genuine when you consider the negligible costs included, the worldwide crowd, and the brief time frame length needed to get the word around.

The Effect That Blogging Has On Affiliate Marketing

Before we dive into the quick and dirty subtleties of how writing for a blog influences the offshoot promoting exertion important to comprehend what these two phrasings involve. This is particularly for the individuals who are as yet green in such matters.

Contributing to a blog is the activity of utilizing a blog also called a web log. As the last name recommends sites are diary like online discussions where individuals post sections which are then successively requested. Numerous web journals are committed to specific theme classes however there are some on which any point can be talked about.

Offshoot showcasing includes the online advancement of the labor and products delivered by given business. A business that claims a site needs to have individuals traffic who would then be able to be persuaded to purchase. The associate showcasing exertion is finished by people for the benefit of the business and these people are named to be 'subsidiaries'. Members utilize a mix of methods to push the advancement plan. A portion of these methods are the utilization of web joins, website streamlining, and through networks. Partners get pay from the business according to the traffic they have coordinated to the site.

Online journals have consistently acquired a lot of prevalence and both offshoot advertisers and web designers have rushed to exploit this reality. Utilizing websites as discussions for notice and advancement is a pattern that subsidiaries are presently embracing notwithstanding the others referenced already. Web engineers have improved things by presenting on the web blog programming that works with more helpful admittance to organizations by means of the subsidiaries. On account of this product 'quack' partners whose aims are to cheat and trick would now be able to be impeded. This has enormously improved the believability of partner showcasing.

Publishing content to a blog has contributed in a huge manner to the achievement of partner showcasing as a methods for online advancement. Using watchwords web crawlers are more equipped for driving intrigued individuals to the significant sites. Dissimilar to spamming which is disapproved of publishing content to a blog isn't as hostile. A famous blog is visited by a lot of individuals in a brief time frame range and by so doing an item or administration is showcased to a serious large crowd. With a crowd of people drawn from everywhere the globe numerous organizations have encountered an upsurge in client volume and obviously main concerns have radically improved. Subsidiary advertising on online journals utilizes watchwords to coordinate traffic. Recordings and photographs are a portion of the extra methods that are utilized to catch the consideration of imminent customers.

The Importance of Mailing Lists in Affiliate Marketing

Mailing records are worthwhile severally. The best thing about having a mailing list is that an individual can robotize a great deal of the interaction by the utilization of an automated assistant. This is an assistance that is offered on the web and it handles the mailings and the mail records for your benefit for a little charge that is paid consistently.

Different administrations incorporate the get reaction and a website admin will likewise give an individual admittance to shape a basic detail that shows up on their site. It ordinarily asks the guests the email address and their names. This empowers a person to tempt the guests to join by giving a free report in return for the data. It prompts them to turn into the individuals from your mailing list consequently. The mailing rundown's significance to the advertiser is huge. A few advertisers have a huge number of names on their mailing records and whenever another item is acquainted with the market, the super advertisers have within track on the business utilizing their capacity to contact their different individuals.

Various individuals look into offshoot promoting as a method of making money or to acquire advantageous pay. The partner showcasing development is certainly not a troublesome undertaking to comprehend since it's anything but an approach to help in bringing in cash from retail items without loading stock, or handle returns if the customer isn't content with the item or make credit deals to the general population.

With regards to subsidiary advertising, the business cycle is totally distant.

When there is no work to be done in accordance with making direct deals, there might be a ton of work associated with making the public mindful of the labor and products you are elevating to them. There are two different ways by which you can draw out your items to general society. One is by buying pay per click publicizing on the fundamental web indexes. You can likewise do this by building a site advancing single or a few items. Exploration uncovers that current buyers are probably going to buy in coming days. This is on the grounds that it is very more straightforward to make a deal to a demonstrated client than to draw in another customer.

The Sure Way to Boost Your Niche Affiliate Marketing Business

Possessing a site has demonstrated to be seemingly perhaps the best approaches to build up an energetic specialty associate advertising business. With this reality there are numerous contemplations that maturing offshoot advertisers take to mind and a large portion of these have to do with the compelled financial plans that they stick to. To possess a site you don't need to burn through every last cent – essentially not until you investigate every one of the choices that are in your domain.

Buying a site is quite possibly the most reasonable choices that specialty member advertisers have available to them. The expenses of getting an instant site regardless, the real factors of the occasions are with the end goal that such a resource can be purchased at well disposed costs. In considering the expense of such an obtaining you need to gauge the importance of the plan to your showcasing exertion. Guarantee that these two angles supplement each other even before you begin arranging. The subsequent thought has to do with the substance on the site. You should guarantee that it is all initially extraordinary – not some simple duplicate glue work.

Buying such a site accompanies extremely helpful benefits. First and foremost, appreciate that we are on the whole gifted in various fields. As a member advertiser you will be unable to make a site all alone and regardless of whether you do it probably won't be as amazing as possible accomplish. The other benefit you will appreciate is the way that a prepared site will empower you to begin showcasing immediately. As an expansion to what exactly has been said on specialization the site will empower you to do what you excel at – promoting – right away. An instant site makes sure that your business vacation isn't excessively drawn out.

There are things that you should likewise check for when making such a buy. You ought to be sufficiently learned to recognize a specialty associate advertising site that you can embrace consistently. The substance in the site should be determined for innovation and here online programming like Copyscape turns out to be truly convenient. You can't simply purchase aimlessly – check the merchant's experience to make certain about their validity. The costs that you bring about in this undertaking may appear to forbid at the beginning however with a helpful site set up for your clients you will appreciate business in the near future.

Composing Quality Keyword Rich Articles for Affiliate Marketing

The utilization of catchphrases in article composing is primarily to accomplish highest level in the different web indexes. Apparently on the off chance that watchwords are the way to getting best positioning, immersing articles with these expressions would be the triumphant methodology. This isn't the situation since doing so has been known to bring about undesired outcomes after scouring the web crawlers.

The motivation behind why this happens is because of the website admin created calculations which decide those articles that are loaded up with significant substance and those that are not. The training at present is to have articles whose catchphrase content makes around 12% of the all out word volume. Articles that are considered to have outperformed these specifications are frequently confronted with the danger of being prohibited. Member advertisers who require SEO articles need not stress since there are a lot of gifted essayists across the globe who are fit for embeddings the right number of catchphrases into an article while guaranteeing that the substance is educational and consistent.

The essential rules for composing SEO articles thusly all have to do with how the necessary expression appropriation is finished. An optimal situation is to have a couple of catchphrases in both the beginning and finishing sections. Every one of the passages in the middle of these two ought to have something like one catchphrase relying upon the length of the article. This may anyway be very precarious when the ideal watchword is difficult to embed by uprightness of its phrasing plan. In such situations article journalists are ordinarily offered the accommodation of utilizing both particular and plural types of something similar.

While composing watchword rich articles it is prudent to continue to peruse the article as it creates and upon its fruition. This is to guarantee that lucidness is kept up with. The best articles are the ones that keep the peruser drew in through and through such that they don't appear to see the rehashed phrases. Of course it is conceivable that the catchphrases are all around dispersed however the center substance isn't instructive. Such an article may breeze through the calculation assessment however will unquestionably slump with the perusers along these lines influencing the deals contrarily.

Despite the trouble that might be available when utilizing catchphrases it will be counterproductive to compel the expression just anyplace. This influences the entire article as understanding the substance gets troublesome. Again this is a valid justification to enlist an expert SEO article author. They do charge some cash however this is effectively recovered from the deals that outcome.

Utilizing Link Building to Market Your Affiliate Website

A few proprietors of online business for the most part the ones who need entire web promoting foundation have an unmistakable advertising plan that acquiring countless connections for their sites is a gainful factor. In genuine sense, completing back the connections when wrongly consequently kills the site. There are a few different ways to return the killed connections to a person's online site. Article advertising enjoys incredible upper hands over different techniques for third party referencing. Different sites proprietors additionally discover joins by sending their locales to various connection catalogs.

On the off chance that you have countless connections on the web, it's anything but an assurance for most web search tools to get your connections and discover their direction to your site. Some online entrepreneurs post their connections on discussions and websites to get customers. These gatherings are very better methods of building joins. This is so in light of the fact that it permits the entrepreneur to associate and bond with others on the web. Others will see, view and react to the remarks. They can likewise surf on your site and see what you offer on it. The strategy can be tedious since it requires some investment to post the discussions and online journals. Yet, it's anything but a ton of time for others to fail to remember your online site.

A few group lean toward article showcasing as the best contrasted with different connections in that article advertisers more often than not gives them space to get their promoting over any remaining third party referencing quick. Through composing great articles, the perusers see them and discover the information or the data that they should impart to other people. For them to discover more, they can simply focus on the connections in the bio boxes about the creators and visit the distributer sites.

Aside from quality traffic and high rankings, article showcasing is likewise profoundly versatile. There is an incredible aggregate impact as numerous articles continue being submitted and supported by the article indexes. In the event that article composing is done completely for about couple of weeks, perusers will peruse and accept the journalists as they can see with their own eyes the commitment endeavors that are normally put by the article advertisers – believable data is the triumphant exertion. Here an individual currently has a few channels. The article advertisers realize how to utilize this strategy to allow others to see them as specialists in that specific field.

Utilizing Social Networking to Market Your Affiliate Site

Interpersonal interaction is one of the techniques for associate advertising systems which can assist you with selling more partner items and administrations on the web. The associate business based at home can be utilized to acquire an assortment of best offshoot advertising techniques which are generally utilized on the web. Site advancement, standard notices, web crawlers and email advertising among others are totally founded on partner showcasing business however there are organizing sites which can likewise be taken as part systems for the locally situated subsidiary business.

Informal communication is the least expensive and easiest locally situated associate showcasing business system alternative that is promptly accessible. Publicizing your locally established associate promoting business is another top member advertising system on the web that can be run without any problem. Interpersonal interaction destinations are basically online spots when you can meet with your customers. By and large, most long range interpersonal communication sites depend on specific subjects and they empower the individuals who share same interests in explicit themes to get together to examine the important issues, give exhortation and pose inquiries among others.

These person to person communication destinations can zero in on any theme. They can likewise zero in on subjects like governmental issues, TV programs, groups, occupations, recent developments, and pastimes or insect possible theme. The partner advertiser can exploit the interpersonal interaction site to arrive at an intended interest group without going through cash. Working at home has gotten progressively famous and there are various sites which center around this specific subject. There are additionally a few systems administration destinations which are engaged and committed to the subject of working at home. Here the gatherings who are keen on this specific point can take the locally established offshoot promoting an open door to present a connection on his site when it's anything but something significant to the discussion. This is best since the person to person communication site include on a high convergence of a person's designated bunch.

With regards to long range interpersonal communication site to advance locally situated partner advertising organizations, it is essential to guarantee that you are following the guidelines related with the social showcasing destinations. The interpersonal interaction destinations now and again may have limitations with respect to the posting of connections and inability to keep the set limitations may cause you to be banished from the informal communication locales. Along these lines, any individual who is keen on utilizing these locales should peruse the client consent to guarantee that they are not abusing any standard.

Week after week, Bi-Weekly, Or Monthly: Which Affiliate Pay Structure Is Best

When searching for a subsidiary program that will be ideal for your web endeavor it tends to be hard now and again. This is a direct result of the unbelievably many partner programs that are offered on the web. Above all else you ought to guarantee that the partner program is trustworthy and has gotten great outcomes for different organizations.

You need to inquire as to whether the program offers leftover profit. This sort of gain is got from profit and is considered as installments gave month to month from each deal. On the off chance that you discover an item that you are prepared to advance and it's from another vendor scan the web for comparable member sourced items. Understand what the program offers, and you keep on providing explicit rates. This offers a person with great data of the deals that the individual will get for a particular decent.

Attempt and select a program that offers limited time assets since it is less complex to advance a thing if there are pennants, locales and adverts that are given at no further expense. It can likewise make your advancement exercises more effortless and significantly easier than you won't ever anticipate. Consider the program that offers a decent compensation structure; attempt to get data concerning the manner in which the offshoot program performs. Assuming you are even the littlest digit befuddled, you should move to the program alternative. Associate projects ought to consistently be in a situation to make it right exactly how their specific program performs.

Try not to pick a program which will expect you to spend anything or requirements you to store a few items. As a member, you become some portion of the company's deal power yet you're utilized uniquely on commission and ought not hold stock. Concoct the leads for your partner by utilizing email pamphlets. A web website is critical generally when you are wanting to produce more money. Find out about an approach to fabricate a work-at-home business and what's needed to make progress. This can sound a basic highlight you if this is your absolute first time giving it a shot. Focus on the elements worried in subsidiary projects. At the point when you follow straightforward advances, these inquiries can turn into much less difficult to find solutions to, and discovering the partner program ideal for your web business will be simple.

Don't miss out!

Visit the website below and you can sign up to receive emails whenever David Steele publishes a new book. There's no charge and no obligation.

https://books2read.com/r/B-A-LHNP-WHLQB

BOOKS 2 READ

Connecting independent readers to independent writers.

About the Publisher

Accepting manuscripts in the most categories. We love to help people get their words available to the world.

Revival Waves of Glory focus is to provide more options to be published. We do traditional paperbacks, hardcovers, audio books and ebooks all over the world. A traditional royalty-based publisher that offers self-publishing options, Revival Waves provides a very author friendly and transparent publishing process, with President Bill Vincent involved in the full process of your book. Send us your manuscript and we will contact you as soon as possible.

Contact: Bill Vincent at rwgpublishing@yahoo.com www.rwgpublishing.com

www.ingramcontent.com/pod-product-compliance
Lightning Source LLC
LaVergne TN
LVHW042004060526
838200LV00041B/1876